IMPERMANENT W

THE CLOSED LINES OF BRITAIN - VOLUME 9

EASTERN COUNTIES

Jeffery Grayer

NOODLE BOOKS

ISBN 978 1 909328 28 0
Printed in England by Berforts, Information Press

First published in 2015 by Kevin Robertson under the
NOODLE BOOKS imprint

PO Box 279, Corhampton, SOUTHAMPTON. SO32 3ZX

www.noodlebooks.co.uk

Front Cover - The former M&GN station at Thorney on the line from Peterborough to Wisbech closed in December 1957 some time prior to closure of the bulk of the M&GN system in March 1959. Today a set of restored crossing gates stand on the site.

Frontispiece - A Gresley rebuild of an original Claud Hamilton design, Class D16/3 No. 62510 stands at Stoke station serving the village of Stoke by Clare situated on the picturesque Bury St Edmunds – Cambridge route with a three coach local on 24th. September 1956. The line closed in March 1967 and a shot of the station after closure can be found on page 70. (Dave Cobbe Collection courtesy Rail Photoprints).

Right - On the 10th. August 1958 an RCTS special, the Northern & Eastern railtour, was run with a variety of motive power. The Class J15 seen here, No. 65440, operated from Marks Tey to Cambridge via Halstead on the Colne Valley route where it is seen during a photographic stop.

Rear cover - "*Very flat, Norfolk*" opines Noel Coward in his play "Private Lives" and whilst not universally true of the county the nature of the geography of East Anglia resulted in a great many level crossings. The guard of a freight working on the Heacham – Burnham Market branch is seen padlocking the nearest set with another set visible in the foreground and a third set in the distance near Sedgeford. This was a time consuming operation for these freight workings which continued for some years after the traditional crossing keepers had been withdrawn following passenger closure. (RH)

The maps on pages 4,10 and 33 are reproduced with the kind permission of the Ordnance Survey. Unless otherwise stated, all images are by the author.

CONTENTS

INTRODUCTION

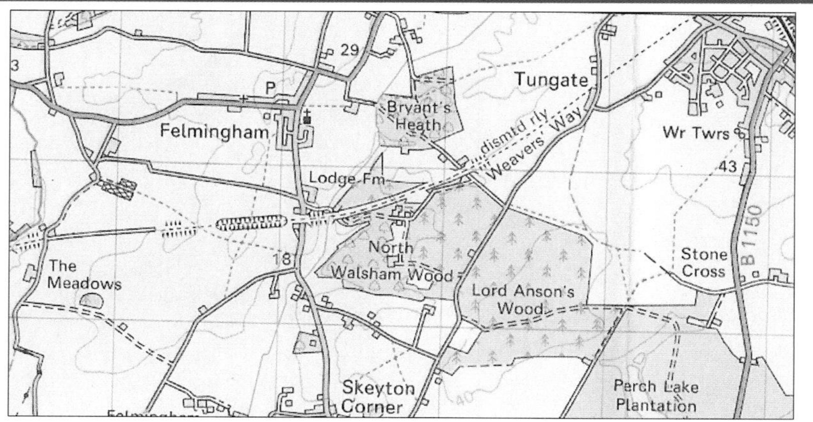

"***Dismtld rly – Weavers Way***" runs the description of the former railway track crossing the extract taken from the OS map alongside. The route once formed part of the sprawling network of the Midland & Great Northern Railway through the eastern counties. Shut controversially in 1959, being one of the largest such closures to that time, parts of the former trackbed have been subsumed into the Weavers Way a long distance footpath which runs for 61 miles between Cromer and Great Yarmouth being named after the once important local weaving industry which flourished in the Middle Ages around North Walsham. Some parts of the trail are available for horse riders and cyclists and attention is drawn in Norfolk County Council's publicity for the route to the variety of former railway infrastructure such as station buildings, crossing cottages and bridges that may be seen. Whilst it is gratifying to know that former railway routes have found a new lease of life, how much more gratifying it would be to see trains back in the landscape on this route. However, this has occurred at many places in the area some of the more significant standard gauge preserved lines being the North Norfolk at Sheringham, the Mid Norfolk at Dereham, the Colne Valley at Castle Hedingham, the Mid Suffolk at Stowmarket, and at Whitwell & Reepham station. Narrow gauge lines laid on former standard gauge trackbeds can be found at the Wells & Walsingham, and the Bure Valley. In addition there is the Audley End Miniature Railway at Saffron Walden with railway museums located at Bressingham, the Wells Harbour Railway, the East Anglian Transport Museum at Carlton Colville and the Mangapps Museum at Crouch End. Many of the views herein were shot on a tour of East Anglian lines taken over 40 years ago in the early 1970s, my own pictures being supplemented by contributions from Mark Shore (MS), Nick Catford (NC) Roger Holmes (RH) and the Railphotoprints (RP) collection to whom, as ever, many thanks.

Jeffery Grayer Devon 2015

Left - A busy scene at Melton Constable hub of the extensive M&GN system. On the 70 ft. turntable, which had replaced an earlier one of 47 ft., is J17 Class 0-6-0 No. 65567 whilst Ivatt Class 4 43156 stands outside the shed. Over 30 Ivatts were allocated to the line from 1951 onwards and they became synonomous with latter day workings. This view was taken on 29th August 1958 some six months before closure of the entire system in February 1959. (Hugh Ballantyne courtesy Rail Photoprints).

KINGS LYNN - HUNSTANTON Closed 5-5-1969

"***Silent miles of wind-bent grasses***" runs a line in the famous Night Mail GPO film of the 1930s and just such a description could be applied here**.** A brisk wind blowing off the nearby Wash ripples the grass grown trackbed at North Wootton, the former level crossing at the southern end of the platform now fenced off under the sightless gaze of the shell of the standard GER signalbox. Not slated for closure in the Beeching report it was hoped that Royal patronage of the line would help to keep the route open but this was not to be and the end came in 1969. In May 2008 the remains of the old signal box were transferred to Leeming Bar station on the Wensleydale Railway in North Yorkshire, the station building having been converted into residential use.

A trio of views of the royal station at Wolferton formerly used regularly by the Royal Family for visits to nearby Sandringham House. In the top picture taken in the early 1970s the former level crossing gates rest against the down platform. (Lower MS)

The crossing gates hang forlornly at Dersingham whose platforms and outbuildings are currently in use as offices and stores for Semba Trading, a builder's merchant, while the main station building has been converted into a private residence. Note the standard GE gabled signalbox situated at the far end of the platform.

BRITISH RAILWAYS

HALF-DAY EXCURSIONS

TO

HUNSTANTON

SUNDAYS

20th JUNE to 5th SEPTEMBER inclusive

OUTWARD JOURNEY			Return fares third class	RETURN JOURNEY (same day only)		
	a.m.	a.m.	s. d.		p.m.	p.m.
Bourne .. .. ..dep.	10 18	..	6/6	Hunstanton .. ..dep.	7 0	7 20
Twenty .. .. .. "	10 26	..	6/3	Heacham .. .. "	7 6	7 26
Counter Drain .. .. "	10 30	..	6/-			
North Drove .. .. "	10 34	..	5/9	Clenchwarton ..arr.	..	8 7
Spalding (Town) .. "	..	10 50	5/6	Terrington .. .. "	..	8 11
Weston .. .. .. "	10 46	..	5/3	Walpole .. .. "	..	8 16
Moulton .. .. "	10 50	..	5/3	Sutton Bridge .. "	..	8 21
Whaplode .. .. "	10 53	..	5/-	Long Sutton .. .. "	..	8 29
Holbeach .. .. "	10 58	..	4/9	Gedney .. .. "	..	8 32
Fleet .. .. .. "	..	11 9	4/6	Fleet .. .. .. "	..	8 36
Gedney .. .. "	..	11 13	4/3	Holbeach .. .. "	8 10	..
Long Sutton .. .. "	..	11 16	4/-	Whaplode .. .. "	8 15	..
Sutton Bridge .. .. "	..	11 25	3/6	Moulton .. .. "	8 18	..
Walpole .. .. "	..	11 31	3/-	Weston .. .. "	8 22	..
Terrington .. .. "	..	11 35	3/-	Spalding (Town) .. "	..	8 53
Clenchwarton .. .. "	..	11 39	2/9	North Drove .. "	8 33	
	p.m.	p.m.		Counter Drain .. "	8 37	..
Heacham .. ..arr.	12 14	12 21		Twenty .. .. "	8 41	..
Hunstanton .. .. "	12 18	12 27		Bourne .. .. "	8 48	..

Hunstanton tickets are available at Heacham

Tickets can be obtained IN ADVANCE at stations offices and usual agents

CONDITIONS OF ISSUE

These tickets are issued subject to the British Transport Commission's published Regulations and Conditions applicable to British Railways exhibited at their stations or obtainable free of charge at station booking offices

LUGGAGE ALLOWANCES are as set out in these general notices

Children under three years of age, free ; three years and under fourteen, half-fares

London, May 1954

Published by British Railways (Eastern Region)   Printed in Great Britain   Stafford & Co., Ltd., Netherfield, Nottingham

HEACHAM - WELLS-NEXT-THE-SEA **Closed 2-6-1952**

Table 39

Table 39 — KING'S LYNN and HUNSTANTON

MONDAYS TO FRIDAYS

Miles		am	am	am C (Commences 1st July)	am B (Commences 15th July)	am C (Commences 22nd July)	am		pm	am	pm	pm	pm (Commences 29th July)	pm	pm M	pm		pm		pm
4	London (L'pool St) dep	..	4 0	6 32	..	7 32	8 36	..	..	1036	..	1236	..	..	2 36	..	..	4 36	..	6 36
8	" (King's C.) "	....	4A 0	6 10	....	....	....	....	....	....	....	....		....	....	....	....	....	....	....
4	Cambridge .. .. "	..	7 57	8 50	..	9 30	9 50	..	..	1150	..	1 50		..	3 50	..	..	5 46	..	8 0
—	**King's Lynn** .... dep	7 18	9 15	10 0	1016	1037	11 3	....	12 10	1 21	2 15	2 58		4 25	5 15	5 54	....	7 0	....	9 8
[illegible]	North Wootton	7 23	9 20	..	..	..	11 8	..	12 15	1 26	2 20	3 3		4 30	5 20	5 59	..	7 5	..	9 13
[illegible]	**Wolferton**	7 28	9 25	....	....	....	1113	....	12 20	1 31	2 25	3 8		4 35	5 25	6 4	....	7 10	....	9 18
[illegible]	Dersingham	7 34	9 29	..	..	1053	1117	..	12 24	1 37	2 29	3 16		4 39	5 29	6 9	..	7 14	..	9 22
[illegible]	Snettisham	7 38	9 33	1020	....	....	1121	....	12 28	1 41	2 33	3 20	....	4 43	5 33	6 17	....	7h18	....	9 26
[illegible]	Heacham	7 43	9 38	1033	1042	1114	1126	..	12 33	1 46	2 38	3 25	4 30	4 49	5 39	6 22	..	7h23	..	9 31
[illegible]	**Hunstanton** .... arr	7 48	9 43	1038	1047	1119	1131	....	12 38	1 51	2 43	3 30	4 35	4 57	5 47	6 27	....	7h28	....	9 36

Heacham was the junction for the West Norfolk Junction line to Wells. Trains on the branch left from the bay platform seen here to the left of this view. The station buildings have mostly survived and, as from 1993, were converted into holiday accommodation, with a camping and caravan site on the old trackbed. A BR Mark 1 first class coach was acquired in 2006 to provide further holiday accommodation. Although the signal box survived for many years it was later removed to make way for a housing estate.

Top - The station building at Stanhoe contains attractive flintwork and still stands today. An old platform trolley adds interest to the scene. This, like many of the stations on this route, was some way from the village contributing to the early demise of the passenger service.

Bottom - Clayton Type 1 D8215 indulges in some desultory shunting en route to Burnham Market in the early 1960s. (RH)

WELLS-NEXT-THE-SEA - DEREHAM Closed 5-10-1964

The steps of the former signal box can be seen are on the left but the remarkable thing is the transformation of the main building into a Russian Orthodox Church and small monastic community house at Walsingham. Today the narrow gauge trains of the Wells and Walsingham Railway stop to the north of the old station site which has a car park on the former trackbed.

Fakenham East plays host to a Class 31 diesel providing a freight service to the mill in the background. Although the station site is now buried under sheltered housing, the Mid Norfolk Railway does hope to return rail services to the town as part of the ambitious North Norfolk Orbital scheme linking Wymondham, Dereham, Fakenham, Melton Constable, Cromer and Norwich.

Looking south at Fakenham East the magnificent set of level crossing gates are a stunning feature of this now vanished scene. In September 1955 the Dereham to Wells and Norwich to Dereham and Kings Lynn lines were turned over to diesel operation, the Wells to Norwich takings increasing by 50%.

County School seen on a very wet day during freight only days. It was built to serve the private Norfolk County School which subsequently changed its name to the Watts Naval School. In 1954 the location was chosen for shooting DMU driver training films for BR. Following the withdrawal of goods traffic from Ryburgh in 1981 the track was removed and the signalbox and island platform buildings demolished. Following a number of preservation schemes involving the Fakenham & Dereham Railway Society, the Great Eastern Railway (1989) Ltd. and ultimately the Mid Norfolk Railway the future of the station is now secure and will hopefully form a link in the North Norfolk Orbital scheme.

Left - To the south of County School lies North Elmham station, also being restored by the Mid Norfolk Railway, which closed to freight in July 1971.

Bottom - The blue BR Dereham Station sign still proclaims the existence of the railway here although by the time of this 1970s shot only freight was carried, the station closing as a coal depot in September 1984. The track was then removed and the station building seriously damaged by fire. However, the Mid Norfolk Railway has undertaken considerable restoration work here and the site re-opened in July 1997. Trains now run to Wymondham Abbey.

KINGS LYNN - DEREHAM Closed 9-9-1968

DEREHAM - WYMONDHAM Closed 6-10-1969

Middleton Towers continues to see freight movements in connection with the local sand quarry, a sand loading silo having been constructed on the line to the east of the station. It was hoped at one time, after a large housing estate had been constructed nearby at Leziate, that the line might re-open to passengers to Kings Lynn but this has so far not happened although a number of charter trains have traversed the line in recent years. Class 67s regularly haul the heavy sand trains.

Typical motive power of bygone days for the sand trains were Brush Type 2, later Class 31 diesels, a green liveried member of which is seen at the station in 1962. The station was named after the nearby stately home, the surviving gatehouse of which was built in about 1455 for Thomas, Lord Scales. (RH)

The Beeching Report intended to retain the Kings Lynn – Dereham - Wymondham line merely closing most of the intermediate stations. However, the whole line was closed and Narborough & Pentney station seen here in the 1970s is now a private house. The station was at one time a temporary terminus of the line from Kings Lynn until the further extension to Swaffham was completed.

A scene of dereliction at East Winch. The signal box seen here lay derelict until salvaged by the Mid Norfolk Railway for use at Thuxton level crossing where, since 2010, it has been resited and restored to working order. The famous cartoonist Osbert Lancaster was a regular visitor here by rail and in one of his books provides the following charming portrait of the station – ***'There is no silence in the world so overwhelming as that which prevails on a small country station when a train has just left it. The fact that it is by no means complete, that the fading echoes of the engine are still clearly audible from the signal box behind which the guard's van is finally disappearing, that one now hears for the first time the cawing of rooks, a distant dog's bark, the hum of the bees in the stationmaster's garden, in no way detracts from its quality.'*** He was a close friend of John Betjeman and illustrated some of the laureate's work and is buried in West Winch churchyard.

Swaffham, former junction for the line to Thetford, boasted an attractive Jacobean style building. The large goods yard and the junction have been redeveloped as an industrial estate although the station building survives. The interior of the building has been renovated forming the Merle Boddy Centre now in use as a community centre.

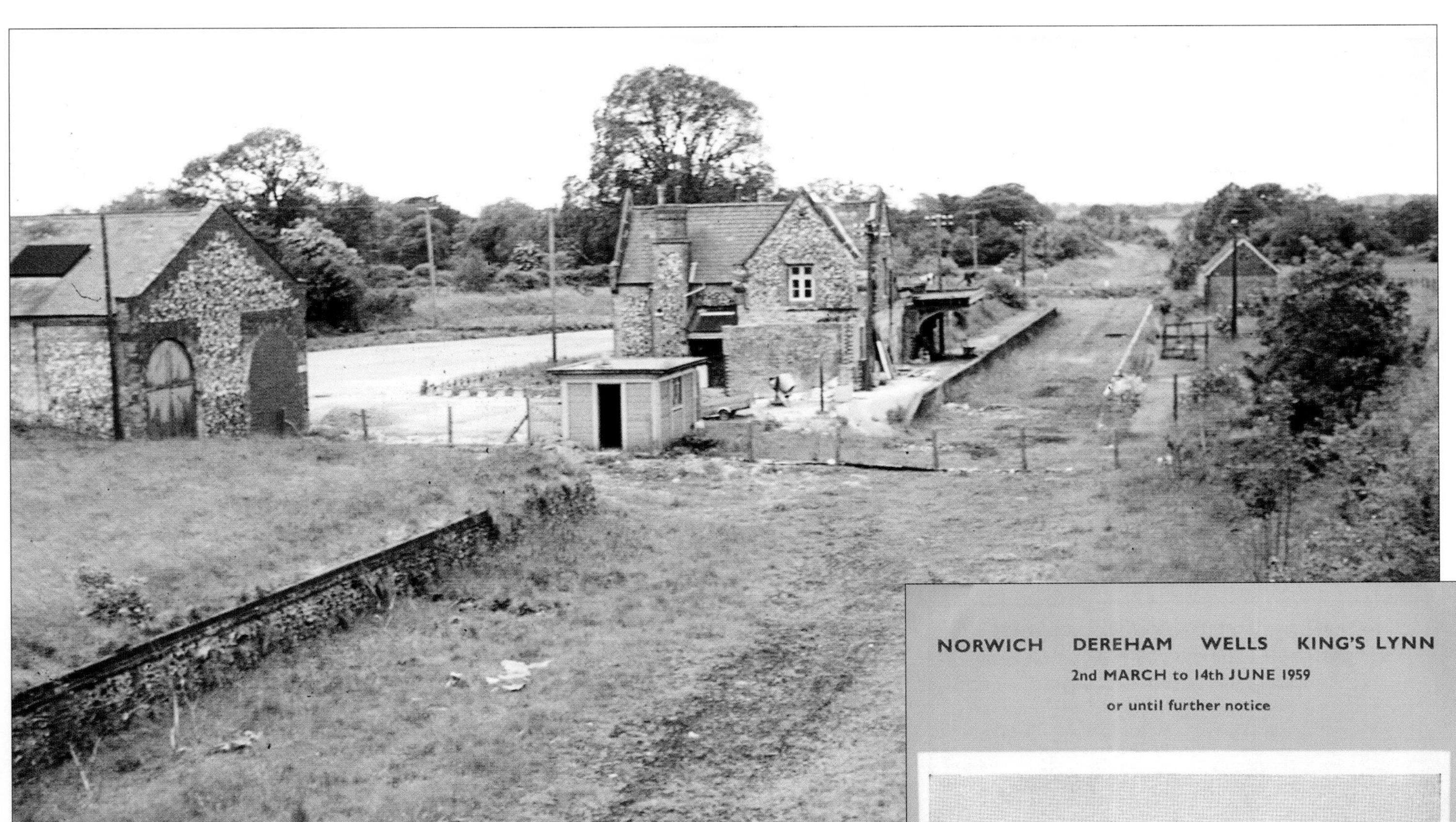

Flint is again to the fore as a building material evident in this view of both the station and goods shed at Dunham. A cement mixer can be discerned on the platform indicative of work to transform the station and although it has now lost its platform canopy the main building has been converted to residential use.

NORWICH DEREHAM WELLS KING'S LYNN

2nd MARCH to 14th JUNE 1959

or until further notice

DIESEL PASSENGER TRAINS

Train services shown in this timetable are subject to alteration or cancellation at short notice and do not necessarily apply at Bank Holidays, Public Holidays or on Race days

E.452

Dereham station looking north this time during its freight only existence witnessed by the goodly number of box vans parked in the bay. Note the modern station lighting evident on the platform it having been expected that the route would survive the cuts of the 1960s.

Although the track has been singled, Yaxham presents a reasonably well cared for appearance in this 1970s view, the box being a particularly fine example of the GER type. Although currently missing its 26 lever McKenzie & Holland frame, it is used as a crossing cabin by the Mid Norfolk Railway which re-opened the station in 1997.

Reepham boasted two stations, that on the M&GN and this on the GER route. It is seen in March 1976 during the time that trains from Lenwade ran through via the Themelthorpe curve. The station now houses a tea room and cycle hire facility, the trackbed here having been turned into a cycleway. (NC)

The sturdy level crossing gates, seen here in newly painted condition, at Cawston are representative of the many hundreds of flat crossings of railways made by roads in East Anglia. The gatekeeper's hut can be seen on the left of this view.

.

Closed 9-9-1968

The rain lashing down into the puddles does nothing to enhance the scene at Smeeth Road which served the village of Marshland St. James. The signalbox seen here together with the adjacent building have both been demolished to make way for residential development although the main station building survives.

4878 2nd - SINGLE SINGLE - 2nd 4878
Smeeth Road to
Smeeth Road Wisbech (East) Smeeth Road Wisbech (East)
WISBECH (EAST)
(E) 1/2 Fare 1/2 (E)
For conditions see over For conditions see over

Class 08 diesel shunter 08 272 passes Coldham gates in the 1970s with a short freight to Wisbech East, a line which continued to see goods traffic until 2000 mainly carrying steel coil for the Metal Box factory and occasional parcels, coal and pet food trains from Nestle Purina. The line was singled in March 1972 with the lifting of the down track. There are plans to restore passenger services from March to Wisbech under the Bramleyline banner however costs of these proposals have recently escalated throwing the viability of re-opening into doubt.

WISBECH HARBOUR BRANCH

Closed 1966

The Wisbech Harbour branch served quays on both banks of the River Ouse and in this 1962 view Drewry diesel shunter D2201, complete with skirts and cowcatcher, traverses a sylvan setting en route to the quay with a couple of wagons and brake van in tow. The first four of these locomotives, (11100-3 later D2200-3) were fitted with side skirting and cowcatchers for use on the Wisbech & Upwell Tramway, still extant at this time, and on the Yarmouth Docks tramway system. D2203, the only survivor of the Wisbech & Upwell Tramway locomotives, is currently operational at the Bolton Abbey & Embsay Railway. The M&GN harbour branch closed in December 1964 with the GER branch closing in September 1966. (RH)

WISBECH & UPWELL TRAMWAY

Closed to freight 23-5-1966

There was never very much by way of railway infrastructure to be found on this famous roadside tramway, and after closure even less so, therefore here are a couple of views of it towards the end of its working life. The first is of D2202 seen at the buffer stops, with a water crane from the days of steam still in situ. The second (below) is taken en route, both views dating from c1962. (Both RH)

A red post box, which no doubt carries the legend "Moulton Station", has been precariously repositioned to a post near the site of the former level crossing. The posts for the former running in board still adorn the platform opposite the substantial station building which has subsequently converted into an attractive house.

Left - Long Sutton's building is of a similar style to Moulton. The green and white sign on the end wall marks the position of a blue enamel sign which formerly read "British Railways Moulton Station".

Bottom - Clenchwarton station's concrete level crossing gate pillars remain in situ in this view.

Almost 20 years after closure the trackbed and platforms at Hillington are being swamped by vegetation. The main station building survives to the present day.

2nd-SINGLE SINGLE-2nd

Melton Constable to

Melton Constable
West Runton

Melton Constable
West Runton

WEST RUNTON

(E) 2/3 FARE 2/3 (E)

For conditions see over For conditions see over

0204 0204

Above - The wasteland that was once the "Crewe of North Norfolk". The locomotive shed built in 1951, with bricked up windows, still survives in this 1970s view as does the former locomotive works seen in the background. Many of the old railway buildings have found new uses, part of the locomotive works apparently being used for potato storage. In 2009 to mark the 50th. anniversary of the last passenger train over the M&GN on 28 February 1959, the North Norfolk Railway brought Midland Railway 4F 44422 to the site on the back of a low loader.

Left - The Central Norfolk Railway, an abortive scheme which never got off the ground, is remembered in these cast iron spandrels which were rescued from the canopy that used to grace the long island platform at Melton Constable station. When the station was demolished in 1971 it was subsequently replaced by a telephone exchange. The brackets now do duty in a humbler role in a local bus shelter. (MS)

Right - The private waiting room, originally provided for the local landowner Lord Hastings who donated the land upon which the station was built, remarkably survives amongst a sea of dereliction. By 1963, with the last remaining service operating to Sheringham and on to Norwich, just 189 passengers in the summer and 166 in the winter used the 10 daily trains then provided to and from Melton Constable with closure of this section expected to produce a net saving of £26,700 p.a. This was clearly an uneconomic proposition and the last service left the town in April 1964. (MS)
Bottom - This 1979 view shows the massive water tanks, built in 1898 and capable of holding 125,000 gallons, which served not only the railway but also provided potable water for the area. It bears traces of repaired shrapnel holes following an air raid in World War 2. (MS)

Above - Hindolvestone with a final "e" according to the M&GN Railway although maps show the village without the "e". Both station and signal box survive in private ownership. The unusual name of the village is believed to derive from the Anglo Saxon *Hildwulfes tūn meaning a* "farmstead belonging to a man called Sword-wolf".

Right - Guestwick was of similar architectural style to the previous station and, like that, both the station building and signalbox survive. (MS)

The Themelthorpe curve was the final section of railway track to be built in Norfolk by BR and was apparently the sharpest curve in the whole of the network. It was opened on 12th. September 1960 to shorten the route of freight trains from Norwich City station and more importantly from the concrete products terminal at Lenwade obviating the need to run via Melton Constable and Cromer. Rails had to be relaid and land which had previously been sold off had to be re-purchased from Reepham, the section from Foulsham to Reepham having previously been lifted. This 1979 view shows the checkrail testifying to the severity of the curve, which was subject to a 10mph speed limit, with the old M&GN route going straight ahead. The M&GN milepost was located between the curve and Whitwell & Reepham station. (Both MS)

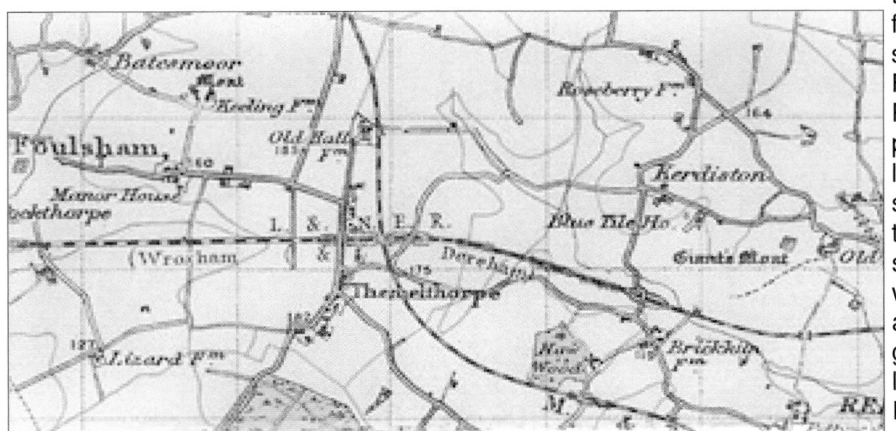

Two views of Whitwell & Reepham the first looking north in March 1976 and the second looking south in September 1979.Following closure, the site hosted various activities including tree surgery, offices, garage and workshop. Norfolk County Council looked at the possibility of making it a travellers' site but in the end it was acquired by Wyatts who intended to establish an alpaca colony. Eventually it was acquired by a rail enthusiast who since 2009 has established a museum, laid track and has the ultimate aim of extending to the Themelthorpe curve and then possibly linking up with the North Norfolk or Mid Norfolk Railways. (Left NC, Lower MS)

Lenwade was the raison d'être for the survival of this branchline long after passenger services had been withdrawn. It is seen here in 1979 with crossing gates, station building and single track still in situ. Today one of the gates still hangs from its post and the building is restored in residential use. The trackbed here forms part of Marriott's Way, named after William Marriott* who served the M&GN for over 40 years in such capacities as Traffic Manager and Locomotive Superintendent, a long distance foot and cyclepath running between Norwich and Aylsham. (MS)

The track from Norwich to Drayton was lifted in 1973 and a trackless Drayton station is evident in this view taken towards the end of the 1970s. The site is now in an industrial park and Drayton has become a suburb of Norwich.

* W G Mariott was also a pioneer in the use of concrete for lineside items. He was probably the first to successfully use concrete for signal posts, something followed later and perhaps not so successfully by the GWR. Marriott would also use concrete for items such as milesposts, as seen on page 33.

Two views of the platforms of the former Holt station and adjacent grain mill, taken in September 1979, now lost under a bypass for the town which hinders any easy extension of the Poppy Line from Sheringham. (MS)

Top - Of double interest is the new station at Holt for not only is it the current terminus of the Poppy Line but it is a reconstruction of the old station at Stalham, also on the M&GN, which was taken apart brick by brick during the winter of 2001/2 and re-erected here.

Bottom - Early days of preservation at Weybourne before the arrival of the footbridge and prior to re-opening in 1975. The station was originally opened as late as 1900 to serve the up market Weybourne Springs Hotel situated on the opposite side of the road to the station and completed about 1902. However, the venture was not a success and following instability in the foundations of the building, which had been constructed upon sand, it was demolished at the start of World War 2.

A pair of views of Cravens 105 DMUs at the formerly named Cromer Beach station. In the upper shot the signalman is receiving the token for the single track line from Sheringham. In the lower a Sheringham bound service waits in the bay platform. The station was renamed plain "Cromer" in 1969. Following the introduction of conductor guard working, ticket office facilities were no longer needed and the building fell into disuse being renovated and reopened as a public house in 1998. The train shed seen here was taken out of use and subsequently demolished the platform being cut back. A large supermarket was built on the site of the goods yards in 1991. A service of purely local trains now operates between Norwich and Sheringham although a single daily through train to and from Liverpool Street from Sheringham via Cromer was introduced in 1997 but it was not heavily used and consequently discontinued.

Aylsham South is now served by the Bure Valley Railway 15 inch narrow gauge line which opened in 1990. It is seen here during its freight only existence carrying rerouted freight traffic from Lenwade via the Themelthorpe curve to Wroxham and Norwich. This traffic finished in November 1981 and the final train was perversely a weed killing special that ran on May 16th. 1983.

A lone passenger shelters from the rain at North Walsham known as Main from 1948 to distinguish it from North Walsham Town the M&GNR station. It is now the only survivor of the pair of stations that served this important market town, the M&GN Town station closing in 1959. This view shows the old enamel running in board still in situ on the far platform together with the operational signal box which was closed following resignalling of the entire line in 2000.

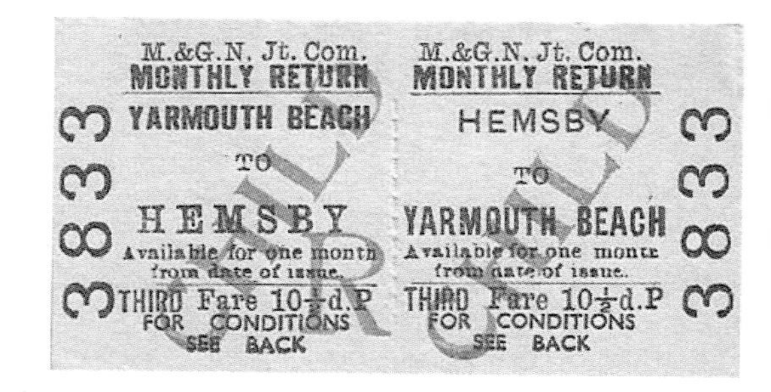

A selection of 1960s/1970s vintage coaches parked up in the pouring rain where trains formerly ran at Yarmouth Beach station which was converted to be the town's coach station in 1962 following closure. It is claimed that up to 1000 coaches were handled here on an August Saturday in 1969. Platforms 2 & 3 on the island remained in use as part of the coach station with Platform 3 having originally extended for 330 yards making it the longest on the M&GN system. The buildings were demolished here in 1986, coach passengers being provided with more modern facilities.

Demolition of the railway infrastructure at Yarmouth Beach was begun with indecent haste just days after closure of the system in 1959. The columns supporting the canopy, which carried the initials EMR (Eastern & Midland Railway) cast in the spandrels, can be seen in this view dating from 12th. September 1979 and today a short length of track on the site is flanked by two of the supports as the only reminder of past glories. (MS)

(18—V19)

MIDLAND & GREAT NORTHERN RAILWAYS
JOINT COMMITTEE.

TO

Yarmouth Beach.

Eye Green was billed rather optimistically as the station "for Crowland Green" some five miles distant. Although in residential use for a time after closure in December 1957 the building was damaged by fire and demolished to make way for the Eye bypass. Freight trains continued to serve the local brickworks until 1966.

Like several towns in the region Wisbech was served by two stations. This is the North station part of the M&GN network which saw goods traffic until March 1964. Taken over by a garage for some years, the station area was cleared in March 1982 for a new housing development, Cricketers' Way.

NORFOLK & SUFFOLK JOINT

Cromer - Mundesley — Closed 7-4-1953
Mundesley - North Walsham — Closed 5-10-1964

Two views of Overstrand's island platform reached by an inclined glazed subway. The station had a working life of just 47 years but was very popular with holidaymakers in the summer months. One famous visitor was the young Winston Churchill who holidayed here from the 1880s and whose final visit was just before the outbreak of war in 1914.

Abbey and West Dereham continued to see freight trains serving the station until 1965 when the section of line from Stoke Ferry to Abbey was closed. The track was removed soon afterwards. The line from Denver to Abbey was relaid in 1971 to take heavier trains and the stretch from Abbey to the British Sugar complex at Wissington was also strengthened. By 1981, however, road traffic to the factory was taking the major part of the load and the line was effectively closed. (Noodle Books Collection)

Old and new motive power at the Wissington sugar beet site. Over 3 million tonnes of sugar beet are currently handled, the factory being supplied by 1,200 local growers. The steam locomotive is a Manning Wardle 0-6-0T named '**Wissington**', the image being taken circa October 1965. Shiny wheel flanges indicate that she is still in use.

An ex-works 0-6-0 diesel seen on the same date, bearing the British Sugar Corporation logo, is undoubtedly a replacement for the steam locomotive.

YARMOUTH SOUTH TOWN - LOWESTOFT

Closed 4-5-1970

Once boasting through services to Liverpool Street, the fortunes of Yarmouth South Town sadly declined after 1959 when it ceased to be the terminus for London trains via the East Suffolk line. It became unstaffed in the mid 1960s with just one operational platform. This view of the rain soaked closed frontage testifies to past glories.

Bottom - The long platforms were latterly served only by the two coach shuttle running to Lowestoft. After closure the station was used as the headquarters of an oil company before being demolished in the 1980s to make way for the A12 link road. A bench from the station, bearing the station name, is however on display at the National Railway Museum, York.

Right - Conversion to DMU operation in 1958 could not ultimately save the line and the final train ran on 2 May 1970. It is seen here with a suitably inscribed headboard preparing to leave, while the driver signs autographs. With the closure of Beach station in 1959 and South Town in 1970 only Vauxhall station remained to serve the town.

Closed 2-11-1959

Top - Seen from Haddiscoe Low level station the embankment in the distance carried the line from Yarmouth to Beccles. The Low level station continues to be served by trains from Norwich to Lowestoft.

Right - A close up view of the signal box above reveals it to be St Olaves Swing Bridge box which controlled the adjacent bridge of the same name, the expense of maintaining the pair of swing bridges over the River Waveney, the other being located near Beccles, being one of the reasons for the closure of this line. The signalbox here has since been extended and converted into a private house.

Vegetation is taking hold at Geldeston. Today it has been converted into an attractive house with the goods shed also surviving. (MS)

A typical crossing keeper's house located near Ditchingham captured in September 1979. Collapsing fencing marks the site of the level crossing. (MS)

Above - A road occupies the site of Ditchingham station today and nothing remains to indicate the presence of the sizeable goods shed and station buildings. (MS)

Right - Looking across the River Waveney towards Bungay station. Here the line crossed briefly into Suffolk before returning to Norfolk. Freight services between Bungay and Beccles lingered on until August 1964. The base of the former water tower can be seen on the right. However, the water tank was saved and taken to the North Norfolk Railway and placed at Weybourne. (MS)

Looking back towards the river, Bungay station is seen in the early 1970s. It was later demolished to make way for the A143 by pass road, rather uninspiringly named 'Old Railway Road'.

River crossing near Bungay seen in 1979. (MS)

Top - Harleston station continues today in use as business premises although unfortunately the road frontage has been somewhat disfigured by an out of keeping extension. (MS)

Left - A conservatory does little to enhance Redenhall station in this 1979 view but today unfortunately a roundabout covers the site. (MS)

Top - Again the A143 has transformed this scene taken in 1979 at Wortwell. (MS)

Right - This is a March 1976 view of Pulham St. Mary station during demolition. Only a gate from the old station, which now functions as a garden gate to an adjoining house, remains today. (NC)

Above - The former overall roof at Aldeburgh station was removed and the signalbox taken out of use before the end of services on the branch which latterly operated as a "basic railway". The conversion to DMU operation in 1956 no doubt prolonged the life of the line. A colourful array of hollyhocks adorns the deserted platform.

Opposite - Aldeburgh station was subsequently demolished and the site used for housing. Removal of the overall roof did nothing for the architectural integrity of the building. Aldeburgh station was subsequently demolished in 1975 and the site used for housing.

ADDITIONAL TRAINS

		a.m.
Saxmundham . .	dep.	8.25
Leiston	„	8.36
Thorpeness (Halt)	„	8.42
Aldeburgh . . .	arr.	8.48

In connexion at Saxmundham with 6.57 a.m. from Yarmouth (South Town) and 7.5 a.m. from Lowestoft (Central).

		a.m.
Aldeburgh . . .	dep.	9.35
Thorpeness (Halt)	„	9.41
Leiston	„	9.48
Saxmundham . .	arr.	9.57

In connexion at Saxmundham with 10.9 a.m. to Lowestoft (Central) and Yarmouth (South Town).

EVERY SUNDAY from 19th August

London, August, 1928.

LNER

Table 28 — SAXMUNDHAM and ALDEBURGH

Miles		Week Days										Sundays							
		am	am	am C	am	pm C	pm	pm	pm	pm		am C	am	am	am	pm C	pm	pm	
	3 London (L'pool St) dep	..	4 35	8 30	9 30	12 30	1 30	3 30	4 50	6 10	..	6†15	8 30	10 10	11 30	2 30	4 30	6 10	..
–	**Saxmundham** ...... dep	6 51	7 49	10 25	11 50	2 34	3 51	5 28	6 52	8 3	....	9 25	10 34	12 13	1 21	4 55	6 33	8 21	....
4	Leiston	7 0	7 58	10 34	11 59	2 43	4 0	5 37	7 1	8 12	..	9 34	10 43	12 22	1 30	5 4	6 42	8 30	..
6¼	Thorpeness..............	7 8	8 6	10 43	12 7	2 51	4 8	5 45	7 9	8 20	....	9 42	10 51	12 30	1 38	5 12	6 50	8 38	....
8¼	**Aldeburgh** . .. .. arr	7 14	8 13	10 50	12 14	2 58	4 15	5 52	7 16	8 27	..	9 50	10 59	12 38	1 46	5 20	6 58	8 46	..

Miles		Week Days										Sundays							
		am	am C	am	pm C	pm	pm	pm	pm	pm C		am	am	pm	pm C	pm	pm	pm C	
	Aldeburgh . .. .. dep	7 20	8 19	10 55	12 20	3 18	4 56	6 18	7 23	8 33	..	10 0	11 40	12 50	2 5	5 36	7 45	8 58	..
2	Thorpeness..............	7 24	8 24	10 59	12 24	3 22	5 0	6 22	7 27	8 39	....	10 5	11 45	12 54	2 9	5 41	7 50	9 5	....
4½	Leiston	7 33	8 33	11 8	12 33	3 31	5 9	6 31	7 36	8 48	..	10 14	11 54	1 3	2 18	5 50	7 59	9 14	..
8½	**Saxmundham** ...... arr	7 42	8 41	11 17	12 42	3 40	5 18	6 40	7 45	8 57	....	10 22	12 2	1 12	2 27	5 58	8 7	9 22	....
99½	3 London (L'pool St) arr	9 54	10 50	1 40	2 50	5 40	7 40	9 7	10 25	11 27	..	12 25	2 50	..	4 50	8 11	10 50	1B 3	..

Tickets from Aldeburgh and Thorpeness are issued on the train

† Second class only between Liverpool Street and Chelmsford | a am | B am. Second Class only | C Through Train from or to Ipswich (Table 3)

Freight trains still operate through Leiston to service Sizewell nuclear power station although the state of the weed strewn track in this 1990 view testifies to their infrequency. Building materials for the construction of Sizewell "A" station during the 1960s and Sizewell "B" station in the 1980s were brought in by rail. "A" station closed in 2006 but a third station "C" is currently under consideration. A siding and gantry crane for handling nuclear flasks was constructed one mile east of the station and trains generally run once a week from Sizewell to Willesden Junction for onward transmission to Sellafield for reprocessing. (NC)

Thorpeness Halt looking rather overgrown in this August 1990 view. Three obsolete GER coaches used to provide the accommodation here in the hopes that the resort might develop but it never took off and, apart from a few patrons of the local golf course, passenger traffic was always meagre and the station became unstaffed in 1962. (NC)

Marlesford station seen from the adjacent A12. The building still stands today in residential use. There were no less than three level crossings in the village and the cost of staffing these no doubt adversely affected the balance sheet of this branch line. A warehouse built on the site of the station yard is currently for sale at £410k (late 2014).

BISHOPS STORTFORD - BRAINTREE

Closed 3-3-1952

Top - Cressing is one of two intermediate stations on the surviving stub from Braintree to the main line at Witham. In this view a dmu approaches Cressing under the watchful eye of the signalman. The box was closed in the 1970s and removed to Castle Hedingham on the Colne Valley Railway. The line to Braintree was electrified in 1977 however passenger numbers from Cressing have declined by more than 20,000 p.a. since 2004 and stand at 29,838 for 2012/13.

Left - Following closure to goods traffic in 1971 and the passage of an enthusiasts' special the following year, rails were removed from Rayne. The trackbed through the old station now forms part of the Flitch Way running between Braintree and Bishops Stortford. Since this 1979 view was taken the station has been restored and after a time as the headquarters of the Essex county park rangers, who maintain the Flitch Way, it now acts as a tearoom popular with walkers. Track was laid, adjacent to the platform in 2013, and this now carries a coach to house a small museum. (MS)

Two views of the attractive station at Takeley, with and without track. The first was taken on 19 July 1972 (MS), the latter in the late 1970s.

LONG MELFORD - BURY ST EDMUNDS

Closed 10-4-1961

LONG MELFORD - SUDBURY

Closed 6-3-1967

Two views of the attractive station at Long Melford. The trackbed in the top image had been considerably tidied by the late 1980s whilst the exterior of the station seen in the lower view shows how the station house was apparently occupied at this time, 1976, whilst the station building itself lies empty. (Exterior view NC)

A view looking south depicts the shell of the signalbox at Long Melford, a downed bridge and the remains of a station trolley make for rather depressing viewing.

Top - The rusting remains of a Vauxhall car, once someone's pride and joy, do nothing to enhance the rural charm of Cockfield which had the suffix (Suffolk) added to its nameboard to avoid confusion with Cockfield in Co. Durham. The station remained open for goods traffic until 1965.

Left - Tracklifting captured near Long Melford featuring a gang of men from the demolition contractor A. King of Norwich with shovels, a crane on hire from Smiths of Bury St. Edmunds and a train of recovered sleepers and chairs.

Although DMUs were introduced to the line in 1959 they could not stem the losses, passenger traffic being very light. A green whiskered 2-car DMU rolls into Cockfield in 1961 where typically staff outnumber passengers. The building survives today in use for solid fuel storage. The cast iron urinal on the right is worthy of note.

A Cravens 105 unit stands at the increasingly decrepit old station at Sudbury in the 1970s. Track layout was reduced to just a single line. The station building was demolished in 1991 to make way for an extension to an adjacent leisure centre which had encroached on the line in stages from the 1980s.

Seen from the north the buffer stops mark the end of the line. The station building housed a local museum for a time. A new station for the town was opened on the site of the old cattle dock in 1991. A £3m investment in the line in 2005 bodes well for the long term future of one of the remaining branchlines in the Eastern Counties and there is a vigorous local campaign to re-open the line north to Cambridge. Passenger figure for 2012/13 show an annual usage of 326,340 passengers.

LONG MELFORD - CAMBRIDGE **Closed 6-3-1967**

Although bereft of nameboards nothing much has changed at Clare station in this September 1969 view, taken a couple of years after closure, other than the presence of weeds on the permanent way. Track was removed the following year. (NC)

Two further views of Clare, taken in October 1973, which now forms part of the Clare Castle Country Park. The station building plus goods shed received Grade II listing in 2013 being the only complete set of 1865 GER station buildings to survive intact in situ. (Both MS)

Top - An interesting contrast with the frontispiece is this view of Stoke station now trackless taken in 1973. One of the station lamps containing the station name is featured alongside. **Left -** The first of two views of Sturmer was taken with track still in situ in September 1969. Note the prominent lamps surrounded by white discs attached to the level crossing gates in the distance. Track was lifted the following year. (NC)

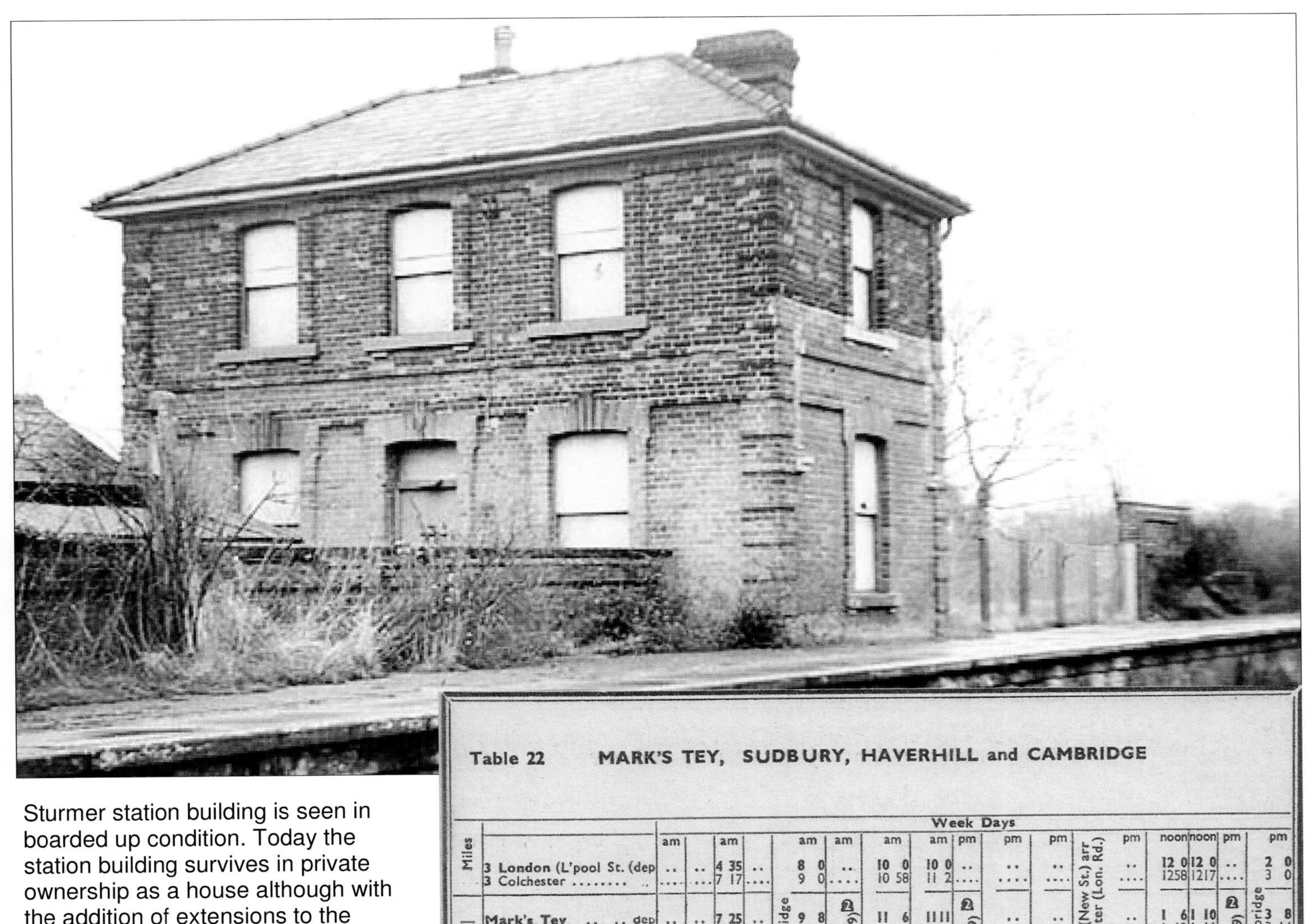

Sturmer station building is seen in boarded up condition. Today the station building survives in private ownership as a house although with the addition of extensions to the original building. (NC)

Table 22 MARK'S TEY, SUDBURY, HAVERHILL and CAMBRIDGE

Miles	Week Days	am		am (Through Train from Colchester)		am (Through Train Colchester to Cambridge)	am ② To Audley End arr 10 54 am (Table 29)	am Except Saturdays; Through Train from St. Botolph's dep 10 51 am	am Saturdays only; Through Train from St. Botolph's dep 10 56 am	pm ② To Audley End arr 12 54 pm (Table 29)	pm Saturdays only	pm Except Saturdays	pm TC Clacton-on-Sea dep 12 12 to Birmingham (New St.) arr 6 20 pm and commencing 10th August to Leicester (Lon. Rd.) arr 5 12 pm (Tables 24, 4, 35, 37); Saturdays only; Commences 29th June	noon Except Saturdays; Through Train from St. Botolph's dep 12 51 pm	noon Saturdays only	pm ② To Audley End arr 2 54 pm (Table 29)	pm Through Train Colchester to Cambridge
	3 London (L'pool St.) dep	..	..	4 35	..	8 0	..	10 0	10 0	..	..	..	..	12 0	12 0	..	2 0
	3 Colchester			7 17		9 0		10 58	11 2					1258	1217		3 0
—	**Mark's Tey** dep	..	..	7 25	..	9 8		11 6	1111		..	..	..	1 6	1 10		3 8
3½	Chappel & Wakes Colne*			7n38		9 14		11 12	1117					1 12	1 16		3 14
6¾	Bures*	..	..	7 44	..	9 21		11 19	1124		..	..	..	1 19	1 23		3 21
11¾	**Sudbury** (Suffolk) arr			7 52		9 28		11 26	1131					1 26	1 30		3 28
	Sudbury (Suffolk) dep	6 30	..	7 55	..	9 29					12 13	1230					3 30
14¾	Long Melford*	6 37		8 2		9d39					12 20	1237					3 36
17¼	Glemsford*	6 42	..		..	9 44					12 25	1242					3 41
18½	Cavendish*	6 46				9 47					12d32	1245					3 45
21½	Clare*	6 52	..		..	9 52					12 37	1250					3 52
23¼	Stoke (Suffolk)*	6 56				9 57					12 41	1255					3 56
26¼	Sturmer*	7 2	..		..	10 2					12 47	1 0					4 2
28¼	**Haverhill** arr	7 6				10 7					12 51	1 5					4 6
	Haverhill dep	7 12	..		..	10 8	10 22			1222	12 52	1 8			..	2 22	4 9
34½	Bartlow arr	7 22				10 18	10 32			1232	1 3	1 18				2 32	4 19
83¼	29 London (L'pool St.) arr	8f52	..		..	..	11b58			1b58	..	..			..	3b58	5 58
—	Bartlow* dep	7 23				10 18					1 3	1 18					4 20
36¼	Linton*	7 27	..	..	..	10 23	..			..	1 7	1 23			..	..	4 24
39	Pampisford*	7 33				10 28					1 13	1 28					
43¼	Shelford A	7 41	..	..	..	10 36	..			..	1 20	1 36	..		..	..	4 36
46½	**Cambridge** A arr	7 47				10 44					1 27	1 42	2 17				4 43
101¼	8 London (King's C.) arr	9 57	..	..	..	12j33	..	..	..	..	..	..	..	..	..	..	7N 5
99	4 „ (L'pool St.) „	9J38															

Week Days—continued | Sundays

Decay is apparent at the once important intermediate station of Haverhill in this view taken in 1969. Demolition followed a couple of years later and after a lengthy period as a derelict cleared site today a superstore marks the spot. (NC)

Two views of Bartlow looking west and east, also taken in 1969, note the former Bartlow Junction signalbox in the distance where the line to Audley End diverged. The station buildings and much of the platforms survive today in residential use with a lawned area now occupying the former permanent way. (Both NC)

Left - The exterior of Linton station seen in October 1973. Today the station building is an office and the stationmaster's house a school. A modern office block has been built on the adjacent trackbed. (MS)

Bottom - Pampisford seen from the adjacent overbridge. The dualling of the A11 road has meant the loss of the complete station site.

Top - All that remained of the Colne Valley station at Haverhill at this time, March 1973, was the platform. Becoming part of the LNER at the grouping, the original CVR terminus saw its trains diverted into the main Haverhill station and became relegated to a goods function. Today a factory car park covers the site. (NC)

Right - After closure and until the mid 1970s, the date of this view, White Colne station was unused and fell into a poor state of repair but it was refurbished and now serves as the village hall. A level crossing separated the station buildings from the platform.

Ashdon station was famous for having a grounded GER coach body acting as a waiting shelter. This was provided in 1916 some five years after local demands for a halt were met. The coach was stripped internally and wooden benches fitted. Remarkably it still lies mouldering today on the vegetation clad timber and clinker built platform.

In March 1957 a new halt to serve the workers at the Coronation Works of Acrow Engineering Ltd on the outskirts of Saffron Walden was opened. The halt was constructed by Acrow and donated to British Railways on completion in 1957. This is the view in September 1969 a couple of years after track was lifted. Today the platform and halt building remain although heavily overgrown and liberally daubed with graffiti. (NC)

Saffron Walden looking north west and seen in November 1969 two years after tracklifting. Today the main station building survives split into two dwellings together with a short length of platform. (Wikipedia Creative Commons:Friendsofnewportstation)

WITHAM - MALDON EAST

Closed 7-9-1964

Formerly the terminus of lines from Witham and Woodham Ferrers, the still impressive Maldon East station is seen in May 1975. The station building still survives and was for many years a restaurant. Although it is largely surrounded by an industrial estate today the grandiose frontage of the building can still be viewed from Station Road. (MS)

Below - By the date of this shot, August 1971 seven years after closure, the overbridge north of Langford & Ulting had been infilled and the platform had lost its rudimentary shelter. Some 15 trains daily in each direction operated over the 5¾ mile branch just prior to closure. (NC)

Right - A surprising survivor was this gradient post on the platform at Wickham Bishops captured in 1975. (MS)

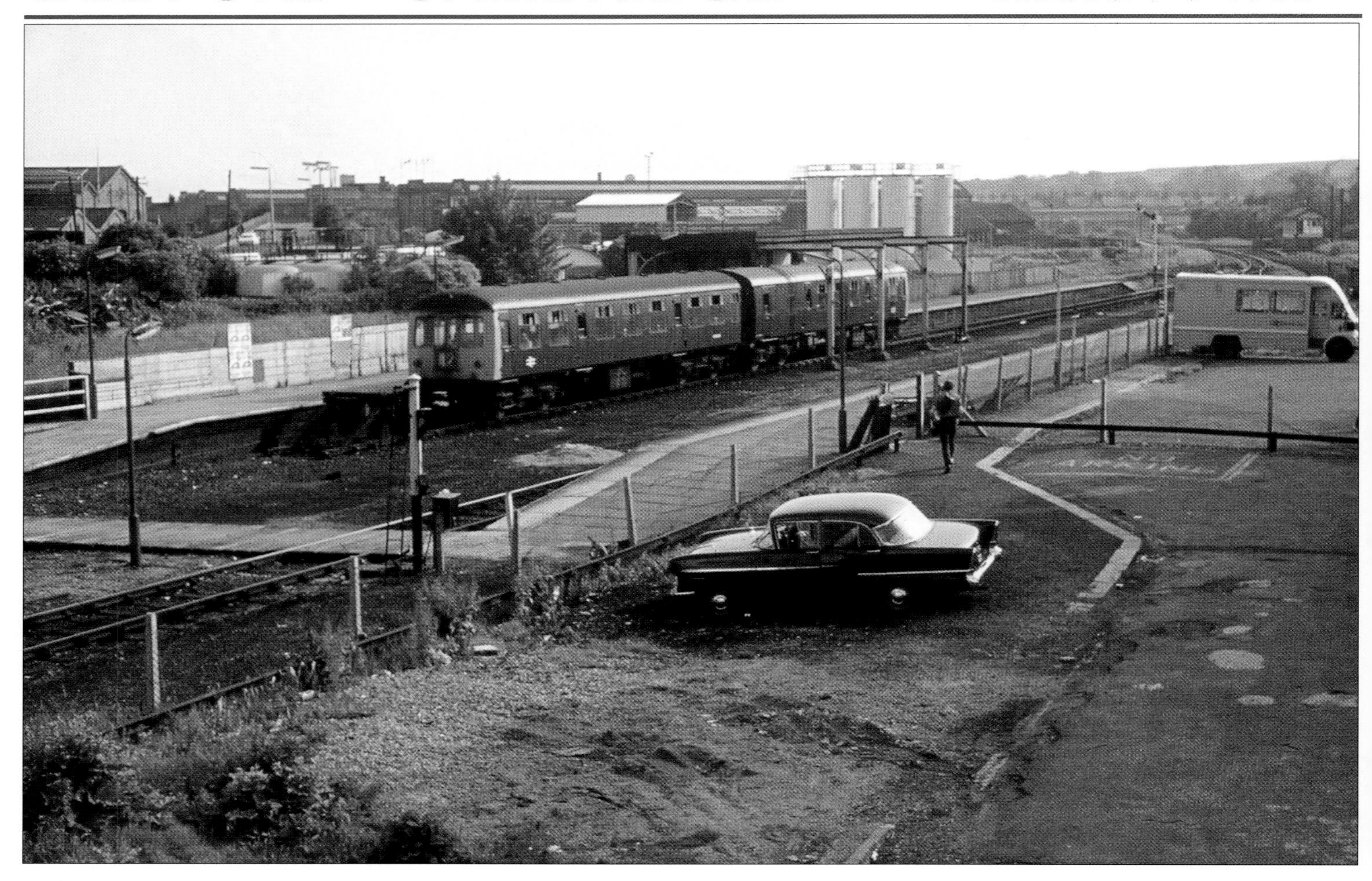

Forty years ago a very basic Bedford St John's plays host to a 2-car DMU, the staple fare on the line from Bletchley. Trains were diverted into the much more convenient Bedford Midland station in 1984 and St John's station resited on the new connecting spur using the old down platform from Fenny Stratford. The old platforms remain, covered in scrub vegetation, and may yet be reused should plans to reinstate the link to Cambridge come to fruition.

Blunham station served a relatively small rural community and coupled with its remote location some way to the south of Blunham village left it susceptible to road competition. This 1970s view shows the station during its derelict phase post closure. Today only the main station building survives as two semi-detached houses surrounded by new residential development.

Sandy was the junction station for the GN mainline and here, in pre-electrification days, a DMU rattles through. The rusting tracks to the left were formerly used by Oxford – Cambridge services. The Bedford and Cambridge platforms were removed in 1975 to allow track quadrupling of the main line.

Seemingly now a timber yard, poppies grow in profusion at Potton station still sporting its glass canopy roof. Track lifting of the Bedford - Cambridge Line began on 13th August 1968. Track was left in place between Potton and Gamlingay pending negotiations for preservation by the Sandy & Potton Steam Railway Society. Unfortunately the Society was unable to raise sufficient funds and the 5¼ miles of track was eventually lifted. The arches on the right were part of the water tower base.

DIESEL
TRAIN
SERVICES

OXFORD, BLETCHLEY
BEDFORD and CAMBRIDGE

WEEKDAYS ONLY

7th SEPTEMBER 1964 to 13th JUNE 1965
(or until further notice)

British Railways
LONDON MIDLAND REGION

Top - This 1970s view of building across the trackbed at Gamlingay station would seem to preclude any chance of re-opening on the former alignment. Today a small industrial estate occupies the site of the goods yard and residential development has occurred elsewhere on the former railway site.

Bottom - Last stop before Cambridge was Lords Bridge. Radio dishes of the Ryle telescope of the Mullard Radio Astronomy Observatory now run on a 20 foot gauge track over the former BR trackbed.

SPOTLIGHT

In each volume we feature one particular station, and in Volume 9 the spotlight falls on - OLD NORTH ROAD

Looking east in the 1970s Old North Road station slumbers on whilst vegetation colonises the former trackbed. Named after the trunk road running nearby, formerly the A14 and now the A1198, this followed the Roman road of Ermine Street.

A colourful view of the signalbox, located near the platform edge for improved visibility, and the station looking west. The box contained 15 levers and was in use until the end of passenger services. The concrete beams of the new overbridge are apparent, the old girder bridge having been replaced a few years before closure.

Top - A Tilley lamp adorns the station nameboard.

Right - With fire buckets and trolleys still in situ, a porter chats to the guard of a Cambridge service prior to departure during the final week before closure. (NC)

Top - The Goods Shed at Old North Road is on the right whilst the platform edge near the building displays evidence of some recent white-lining. Nearest the camera the edge line is broken and of the style adopted at many stations during WW2. Whether this remains a throwback to that period is uncertain although what is likely is that the solid line adjacent to the main buildings was used as an indication to the driver of where the then two-car DMU service should come to a stop.

Conversion into a house is obviously in full swing in this view taken in March 1976. (NC)

ST. IVES - CAMBRIDGE

Closed 5-10-1970

Taken some three years after closure the impressive junction station of St Ives survives albeit in a boarded up state. After earlier closures, only services to Cambridge survived until the end. The buildings were demolished about 1980.

The track to the left, now terminating at the buffer stops, formerly extended to Huntingdon but services were withdrawn in 1959. The platforms on the right formerly served the lines to Ely, closed 1931, and to March, closed in 1967.

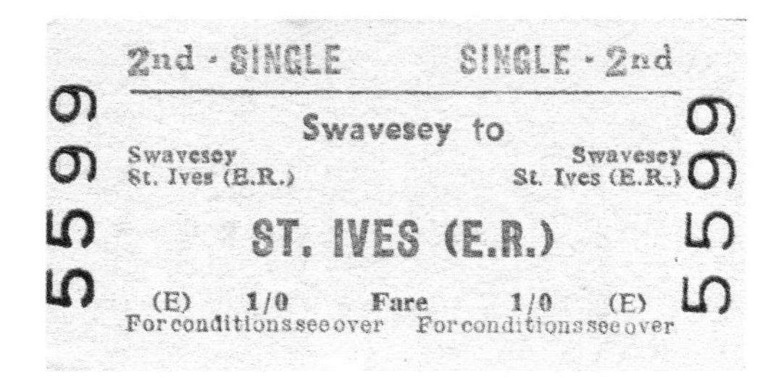
2nd · SINGLE   SINGLE · 2nd

5599   5599

Swavesey to

Swavesey St. Ives (E.R.)   Swavesey St. Ives (E.R.)

ST. IVES (E.R.)

(E) 1/0 Fare 1/0 (E)

For conditions see over   For conditions see over

Swavesey station seen a couple of years after closure. The station remained derelict until it was demolished in the winter of 2007/8, timed apparently to avoid the bird nesting season! This destruction was in connection with the provision of the Cambridgeshire Guided Busway, a controversial scheme linking Cambridge with St. Ives and Huntingdon, which utilised the trackbed of the old railway in part. Specially adapted buses are used with the driver not being required to hold the steering wheel on the guided sections. A total of 2½ million trips were made in 2011, the first year of operation. Overruns have seen costs spiral to close on £200 million leading many, including the Cambridge MP, to brand it an expensive “white elephant”.

Becoming unstaffed in March 1967, Long Stanton again survived until demolition of one platform in 2007 although parts of the platform were rescued for re-use on the Mid Norfolk Railway. The station building and the other platform remain alongside the new guided busway.

The station building remains today as a private house at Oakington although the St. Ives platform has been demolished.

Weeds are beginning to colonise the track in this early 1970s view. The local community managed to save Histon station from demolition in 2008, although the platforms have largely disappeared, and ideas are currently being sought for the site's future use.

ST. IVES - MARCH

Closed 6-3-1967

Staggered platforms were provided at Chatteris as seen in this view. Freight was withdrawn in April 1966 with passenger services ceasing the following March. In the 1960s some 80 trains were timetabled through here daily and it was an important diversionary route seeing some famous expresses such as the *Flying Scotsman* and the *Aberdonian* pass through. New rail technology including concrete sleepers, continuous welded rail and multiple aspect signalling, was also trialled on the line.

Right - This exterior view shows the porticoed entrance to the substantial station building. The station was demolished in the 1970s and the A141 built on the formation.

Bottom - Part of an old coach body adorns one of the platforms next to the Waiting Room.

Two views of Stretham in which the grass grown trackbed of the first shot has been transformed into a productive crop growing area in the second 1976 image. Only the far building with canopy now survives at this location, a new house having been constructed on the rest of the site. (Lower NC)

Top - Wilburton seen in March 1976. Although the main building still stands it has been incorporated into a much larger house and is now difficult to identify as being of railway origin. (NC)

Right - Bluntisham seen in the early 1970s has now been converted into a dwelling. Goods traffic continued here until October 1964 and the occasional passenger service for fruit pickers and annual excursions to coastal resorts ran until the late 1950s.

CAMBRIDGE - FORDHAM - MILDENHALL

Closed 18-6-1962

Rattling through Fordham station under clear signals with a service to Ely is a 2-car green whiskered DMU. The line branching off to the right is the Mildenhall branch. Fordham closed to passengers three years after the Mildenhall line but trains still pass through running from Ipswich to Ely.

The wooden station building at Quy, pronounced Kwai, an intermediate station between Cambridge and Fordham, still survives today.

Isleham was situated between Fordham and Mildenhall. The Mildenhall branch was a pretty dire scenario economically speaking and in 1955, in the steam era, a passenger receipts / movement cost ratio was recorded as being a miserable minus 93%. Even dieselisation could not turn round such a hopeless case and merely postponed inevitable closure for a couple of years.

Two views of Mildenhall terminus with a DMU waiting to depart with one of the handful of daily services. Today the station, platform and goods shed all survive.

Braughing, locally pronounced Braffing, seen some 10 years after closure. The son and grandson of the last stationmaster have now transformed the building into a desirable dwelling and a length of track and coach now grace the platform. Occasional open days are held.

SOMERSHAM - RAMSEY EAST **Closed 22-9-1930**

In the early 1970s Somersham was moribund awaiting a new but at the time unknown future. The contractors had lifted the track through the station although out of camera shot a vestige of track remained where a boarded crossing adjacent to the station level crossing was sited. The wooden building was later carefully dismantled and re-erected as part of Sir William McAlpine's private railway.

Freight continued from Somersham to Warboys station until 1964. Today the platform ramps can still be made out but the remainder of the station has been buried.

HOLME - RAMSEY NORTH

Closed 6-10-1947

Rails are still shiny at Ramsey North terminus. It closed to freight in July 1973 and in 1974 the buildings were demolished and the site cleared. Ramsey Auction Rooms now occupy the site. Ramsey was unusual in being the site of two termini of branchlines, the other running from Ramsey East to Somersham and closed to freight in 1956. Plans to join them never came to fruition.

St Marys was an intermediate station on the branch and this view dates from March 1976. Following passenger closure as long ago as October 1947, goods continued to run to Ramsey North although the station was downgraded to an unstaffed public siding in May 1960. Following the withdrawal of freight services in about 1971 this insubstantial platform was later demolished and housing now occupies the site. (NC)